The Christmas Theme Pack

for Upper Primary

Written by Ron Shaw

Published by Prim-Ed Publishing

Foreword

Having its origins in the tiny towns of Bethlehem and Nazareth 2000 years ago, Christmas is now celebrated all around the world.

It is both a time of joy and a time for reflection; it is sharing, forgiving, a time for hope. For millions upon millions, Christmas means peace, goodwill and charity. It is a time when families become even closer, when strangers say 'Hello'.

In this book we have endeavoured to provide teachers and students with a range of Christmas-related activities, keeping in mind the dual themes of joy and peace.

We trust your students are stimulated and challenged by the pages that follow.

Contents

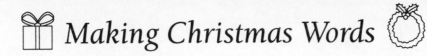

Making Christmas Words

How many Christmas points can you get by making Christmas words? Each letter of each correct word earns one point. *(All words must be spelt correctly so have your dictionary ready.)*

Words of Four Letters

Total: _____

Best Score: _____

Achieved by: _____

Words of Five Letters

Total: _____

Best Score: _____

Achieved by: _____

Words of Six Letters

Total: _____

Best Score: _____

Achieved by: _____

Words of Seven Letters

Total: _____

Best Score: _____

Achieved by: _____

Words of Eight Letters

Total: _____

Best Score: _____

Achieved by: _____

Words of Nine Letters

Total: _____

Best Score: _____

Achieved by: _____

Words of Ten Letters

Total: _____

Best Score: _____

Achieved by: _____

Words of Eleven Letters

Total: _____

Best Score: _____

Achieved by: _____

Words of Twelve Letters

Total: _____

Best Score: _____

Achieved by: _____

My Grand Total of points: _____

The Best Class Score: _____

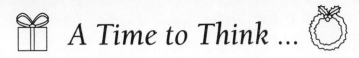

A Time to Think ...

Most of us are lucky to enjoy Christmas Day, spending it with family and friends, enjoying good food and receiving presents. Unfortunately, there are lots of people around the world who are not so lucky. Discuss the following passage and answer the questions.

The sun rises slowly above the flat horizon. Barren fields stretch forever in all directions; a few lifeless trees serve only to add to the starkness of this forbidding country.

The dull thud of exploding grenades can be heard from afar.

A tiny child, painfully thin, mumbles feebly to her distraught mother. The child is hungry. She was hungry yesterday; last week; last month. She has been hungry all her life ... 6 years.

Her sad, black eyes are devoid of hope. Her mother's are the same. Dirty, unwelcome flies have settled on the girl's mouth and nose ... they'll be there for the day, again.

This is just another day in Rwanda, Africa. Somehow, though, today is even sadder than yesterday. Today is Christmas Day.

1. Provide meanings for the following words.

    (a) barren _____

    (b) stark _____

    (c) forbidding _____

    (d) feeble _____

2. Rwanda is experiencing 'the horrors of a double tragedy'.

    What do you think this means? _____

    _____

    _____

    _____

3. Why is the girl's mother distraught? _____

    _____

    _____

4. Explain 'devoid of hope'. _____

    _____

5. Is it good to think about Rwanda and its troubles at Christmas time?

    Why or why not? _____

    _____

    _____

    _____

    How could you help the Rwandans? _____

    _____

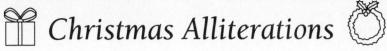

Christmas Alliterations

Complete these alliterations using as many Christmas words as you can. Make them amusing Christmas sentences - the funnier the better!

One wishful wife _____

Two tall trees _____

Three thin threads _____

Four frilly fairies _____

Five frosty firs _____

Six silly snowmen _____

Seven singing santas _____

Eight amazing angels _____

Nine naughty nannies _____

Ten terrible toys _____

Eleven embracing elves _____

Twelve terrific turkeys _____

Use the following Christmas words and make up your own funny alliterations.

Bethlehem, mistletoe, reindeer, yuletide, sleigh, Christmas carols, glitter, presents, star, manger, stocking, December, Jesus, goodwill, holly, pudding, gifts, shepherds, peace

_____

_____

_____

_____

_____

_____

_____

_____

_____

The Real Meaning of Christmas - Why We Celebrate

According to the Gospels of Saint Luke and Saint Matthew in the New Testament, an angel appeared to shepherds near the town of Bethlehem about 2000 years ago. The shepherds were told of the birth of Jesus.

Jesus' mother was the Virgin Mary, her husband was Joseph. When Joseph discovered that Mary was pregnant, an angel appeared to him in a dream. Joseph was told that Jesus was a child of the Holy Spirit.

Mary and Joseph had originally lived in the tiny town of Nazareth. They had gone to Bethlehem to record their names in a census. When in Bethlehem, Mary made a cradle for Jesus in a manger, after first finding shelter in a stable.

Soon after Jesus' birth, three wise men from the east followed the light of a star to Bethlehem. When they arrived they gave gifts to Jesus. The gifts were gold, frankincense and myrrh. Mary and Joseph returned to Nazareth with baby Jesus shortly after the birth.

Answer each question in one or more complete sentences.

1. Why do you think there are certain details of Jesus' life that are not too certain (e.g. exact date of birth)? _____

   _____

   _____

   _____

2. What is a probable reason that Mary and Joseph could not record their names in a Nazareth census? Why did they need to go to Bethlehem?

   _____

   _____

   _____

3. Why were Mary and Joseph staying in a stable?

   _____

   _____

4. Why did the three wise men bring gifts to baby Jesus?

   _____

   _____

5. After reading the above passage, it is clear that the birth of baby Jesus was quite different from that of babies in modern cities. In what ways was his birth different?

   _____

   _____

   _____

Christmas Jumbled Cloze

Unjumble the following lists of words and use these to complete the Christmas cloze.

nbirbso _____	lone _____	melhteebh _____
ymifla _____	tlesab _____	lnwsboal _____
rtehe gikns _____	figts _____	aahzetnr _____
aksc _____	soty _____	tieostmle _____
namwson _____	cepae _____	shacimrts rete _____
tleitgr _____	asnat _____	ligshe _____
tcigsokn _____	yoj _____	nodarcisoet _____
safet _____	alrsoc _____	isltne _____
lebls _____	nwos _____	enerride _____

We were singing 'The First _____' and other Christmas _____. The

_____ _____ looked very pretty with the lights and its glittering

_____ and all the other _____ we had put on it.

Little bits of sparkling _____ had settled on some of the _____ which had

been carefully wrapped with colourful _____.

Sam was hoping that his _____ would be full of _____ in the morning. In

just a few hours _____ was due to arrive with his _____ pulling him

along on his _____. We were all planning on listening to the jingling _____

and we hoped Santa's _____ of toys would be full.

As Dad put up the _____, Toni and the other girls ran outside to play in the

_____. They wanted to see who could make the best _____ and the

largest, roundest _____.

Everyone was hungry. Mum had prepared a real _____ for the _____ to eat.

As we sat down to enjoy our meal, my thoughts drifted to the real meaning of Christmas. I

remembered the story about the _____ _____

who followed a star to a small _____ in

_____. Jesus of _____ is the reason

for all Christmas celebrations and _____ on earth

was his wish; this is the real _____ of Christmas.

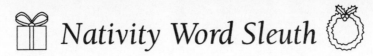 # Nativity Word Sleuth

Find the following words hidden in the word sleuth below.

evening star	Herod	donkey	angel
Three Wise Men	manger	Messiah	worship
New Testament	baptised	disciples	Galilee
frankincense	myrrh	kings	Gold
Matthew	Luke	lamb	son
shepherds	Jewish	Judea	Jesus
Mother Mary	Joseph	Bible	gospels
Bethlehem	Passover	stable	Nazareth
Advent	Inn		

H	D	E	V	E	N	I	J	M	E	H	E	L	H	T	E	B	G
E	M	O	B	M	L	L	O	T	H	E	L	E	G	N	A	A	A
H	E	A	N	I	A	B	W	O	R	S	H	I	P	M	M	P	P
S	S	Y	N	M	B	N	A	B	I	B	J	F	D	O	A	N	A
T	S	E	B	G	O	L	D	T	O	A	R	R	I	T	T	E	S
N	I	K	O	R	H	T	E	J	S	A	A	S	S	H	T	M	S
N	A	N	J	O	S	E	P	H	N	T	H	N	C	E	H	E	O
I	H	O	O	E	B	E	T	K	S	E	A	S	J	R	E	S	V
T	N	D	S	B	W	J	I	G	P	D	H	E	S	M	W	I	E
S	D	E	M	I	W	N	N	H	V	E	S	S	A	A	E	W	R
L	M	O	W	B	C	I	E	E	S	U	G	E	J	R	E	E	J
E	E	N	R	E	N	R	N	E	S	N	D	M	E	Y	L	E	S
P	S	O	N	E	D	T	H	U	I	U	P	E	W	P	I	R	E
S	S	S	V	S	H	S	D	K	J	S	C	S	I	D	L	H	K
O	E	E	D	S	E	L	P	I	C	S	I	D	S	H	A	T	U
G	Z	M	Y	R	R	H	M	A	N	G	E	R	H	S	G	M	L
H	A	D	S	M	T	N	E	M	A	T	S	E	T	W	E	N	N
S	N	A	Z	A	R	E	T	H	N	D	E	S	I	T	P	A	B

Work out the following mathematical code and then solve the following message.

A	B	C	D	E	F	G	H	I	J	K	L	M	N	O	P	Q	R	S	T	U	V	W	X	Y	Z

A = (4 x 3) x 2   B = (A ÷ 6) x 2   C = 144 ÷ [48 ÷ (6 x 2)]

D = 75 ÷ (12 ÷ 4)   E = 105 ÷ (7 x 5)   F = (E x 9) ÷ 3

G = [(6 x 3) ÷ 2] + (54 ÷9)   H = (24 - 15) + (3 x 4)   I = (H - G) ÷ (21 -G)

J = 11 + 10 + 9 + 8 + 7   K = (33 ÷ 11) x (42 ÷ 7)   L = (C + K) ÷ 2

M = (12 - 10) x (4 ÷ 2)   N = (100 ÷ 4) ÷ (16 - 11)   O = (B + M) ÷ (N - E)

P = (9 ÷ 9) x (63 ÷ 9)   Q = (50 - 30) ÷ 10   R = N x Q

S = (18 -11) + (12 ÷ 3)   T = 1 000 ÷ [(6 x 5) - 10)]   U = (L ÷ F) + F

V = Q x E x N   W = (H ÷ P) x (P + Z)   X = [(W - T) x R] ÷ N

Y = 80 ÷ (B ÷ M)   Z = (2 x 9) - (25 ÷ 5)

50 • 21 • 3   4 • 6 • 11 • 50   1 • 4 • 7 • 6 • 10 • 50 • 24 • 5 • 50

___ ___ ___   ___ ___ ___ ___   ___ ___ ___ ___ ___ ___ ___ ___ ___

50 • 21 • 1 • 5 • 15   24 • 50   36 • 21 • 10 • 1 • 11 • 50 • 4 • 24 • 11

___ ___ ___ ___ ___   ___ ___   ___ ___ ___ ___ ___ ___ ___ ___ ___

50 • 1 • 4 • 3   1 • 11   50 • 6   11 • 7 • 10 • 3 • 24 • 25

___ ___ ___ ___   ___ ___   ___ ___   ___ ___ ___ ___ ___ ___

15 • 6 • 6 • 25 • 60 • 1 • 27 • 27

___ ___ ___ ___ ___ ___ ___ ___

Using the same code, make up your own Christmas message, then give it to a friend.

_____

_____

_____

_____

_____

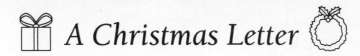 # A Christmas Letter

You received this letter from your new penfriend Lisa in Canada, describing how her family celebrates Christmas. Write a reply explaining how your Christmas celebrations are different. Be clear and concise in the letter but be sure to cover all aspects.

Dear _____,

Thanks for your letter and the photo of your family, which I received on the 9th of December. It was nice of you to tell me about your family and friends. What an interesting life you have!

Everybody over here is getting excited as Christmas approaches. Yesterday we watched a Christmas parade featuring the Royal Canadian Mounted Police. They looked great in their colourful uniforms and the horses were in beautiful condition.

Santa followed on, just behind the Mounties. He was being pulled along in a sled, with two of his elves. As the elves waved and jingled bells Santa held up a large Canadian flag which, as you know, features a red maple leaf on a white background.

The whole thing looked quite spectacular, especially when they passed the gigantic CN Tower, one of the world's tallest structures. The weather was perfect; not a breath of air but crisp and fresh (pretty freezing to be honest!). We were lucky to have only a light snow fall during the parade. The trees lining the street looked super with their snow-covered branches.

Tomorrow, Sunday, my family is going to the Rocky Mountains where we hope to do some skiing and tobogganing. We'll go fishing in the mountain streams with Dad and probably skate on the frozen lake. The best part will be sitting in front of the cozy fire in our log cabin. It's nice and warm after being in the snow all day.

Merry Christmas, and please write soon and tell me about your Christmas.
Your friend,
Lisa

Dear Lisa,

_____

_____

_____

_____

_____

_____

_____

_____

_____

_____

_____

_____

In the *British Isles,* many people go from house to house singing Christmas carols. This tradition began many years ago when visitors sang carols for a drink from the wassail bowl, which contained a hot punch made from ale, apples, sugar, eggs and spices. Christmas carols were introduced in the 1600s, and in the 1800s words were put to the music. In *Great Britain,* carolers can be seen singing the festive tunes in public places. In *Wales,* they have carolling contests in the weeks before Christmas.

In *Ireland,* people put a lighted candle in their windows on Christmas Eve to welcome passing travellers. The hanging of mistletoe in the home originated with the Celtic priests' ceremonial use of giving gifts of the sacred plant.

In *France,* children put their shoes in front of the fireplaces so Pére Noël (Father Christmas) can fill them with gifts. Many families have a festive supper called 'Le réveillon' after attending midnight mass.

In *Sweden,* the Christmas season starts on 13 December, St Lucia Day. The eldest daughter dresses in white and wears a wreath with seven candles on her head, bringing her family coffee and buns. Children believe that a lively elf, Jultomten, bring them gifts on Christmas Eve, from Santa Claus.

In *Germany,* children receive sweets on 6 December from Saint Nicholas, who also collects the childrens' wish lists for their gifts. Saint Nicholas was a Christian Bishop who died in the AD 300s. Christmas presents are received on Christmas Eve by Weihnachtsmann (Christmas Man); they come from the Christkindl (Christ Child).
Germans decorate their homes with Christmas trees, a tradition that originated in medieval Germany in the 1600s. Then families decorated evergreens with fruit, nuts, candy, painted eggshells, paper flowers and lighted candles.

In *Spain,* people dance and sing in the streets after midnight mass on Christmas Eve. A miniature Nativity scene is displayed in most Spanish homes and churches; this scene of the birth of Jesus is called a Nacimiento.
Spanish children on the eve of Epiphany (the last day of the Christmas Season) place their shoes near a window. The Magi, the Wise Men, come and fill them with small gifts, just as they bore gifts to Jesus in Bethlehem.

In the *Netherlands,* children are given presents on the eve of 6 December. According to legend, the gifts are brought by Saint Nicholas who, wearing a red robe, arrives on a boat from Spain and rides down the street on a white horse. His servant, Swarte Piet (Black Pete), accompanies him.

Christmas Questionnaire 1

Using these passages and your own research, answer the following questions.

What is something that Christmas celebrations in France and Spain have in common?

_____

_____

_____

Who was Saint Nicholas? Mention at least two countries in which Saint Nicholas features prominently in Christmas celebrations.

_____

_____

_____

What is the difference between Santa Claus and Saint Nicholas? List any other people who reward children with presents at Christmas time.

_____

_____

_____

What is the significance of Christmas decorations such as holly, Christmas trees and wreaths being red and green? What do the colours represent?

_____

_____

Tell all you know about the wassail bowl.

_____

_____

_____

_____

Who is Swarte Piet?

_____

Who is the Christkindl?

_____

What are the holidays leading up to Christmas Day? In which countries are they celebrated?

_____

_____

_____

Find out where and when Christmas carols originated.

_____

_____

In the *United States and Canada,* a traditional Christmas dinner consists of mashed potatoes, stuffed turkey, roast goose or ham, cranberry sauce, and a range of other dishes. Plum pudding, fruitcake and pumpkin pie are among the favourite desserts.

Many families have Advent wreaths of holly and evergreens, with four candles; one candle is lit on each Sunday of Advent to mark the 24 days to the coming of Jesus on Christmas Day. Advent calendars also track these days, having small doors with celebration pictures and messages behind them.

In *Italy,* the family prays on Christmas Eve while the mother places a figure of the Bambino (Christ Child) in the manger. A Christmas bread called panettone, containing raisins and fruits, is baked as dessert. Italian children receive gifts from La Befana, a kindly old witch believed to be searching for the Christ child. Hanging a Christmas wreath on the front door is believed to have begun with the decorative wreaths in ancient Rome used as a sign of victory and celebration. Many are made from evergreen leaves and holly, with its red berries.

In *Poland,* people attend Pasterka (Shepherd's Mass) at midnight on Christmas Eve. Many Polish families follow the Christmas tradition of breaking an oplatek, a thin wafer made of flour and water. The head of the family holds the wafer, and each person breaks off a small piece and eats it.

In *Denmark,* Christmas dinner includes rice pudding called Julgröt, which has a single almond in it. Tradition says that whoever gets the almond will have good luck throughout the coming year. Danes believe that a lively elf called Jukenison brings them gifts from Santa.

In *Australia* and *New Zealand,* Christmas comes in summer. Many people go to the beach or have a picnic for their Christmas celebrations. They enjoy their traditional Christmas dinner cold. School children have a six-week summer holiday at Christmas time.

In *Mexico,* the nine days before Christmas have special importance. These days are called posadas, which means 'inns' or 'lodgings'. On each day, Mexicans re-enact Mary and Joseph's search for lodging on the first Christmas Eve. Two children carrying their figurines lead a procession of people to a particular house seeking lodging. At first they are refused but are later admitted.

In *Asia* and *Africa,* the celebration of Christmas is not widespread because relatively small numbers of Christians live in these continents. However many western customs are followed; religious services are attended, people exchange gifts, carols are sung, Christmas trees are decorated and Santa Claus is present.

Christmas Questionnaire 2

Using these passages and your own research, answer the following questions.

What is panettone?

_____

_____

Why is Christmas in Australia and New Zealand much different from Christmas in the other countries mentioned?

_____

_____

_____

Why is it lucky to eat Julgröt? Find another country with a similar tradition.

_____

_____

Describe the Polish Christmas tradition surrounding the oplatek.

_____

_____

_____

_____

Is it true that, in one country, it is believed that a witch brings presents at Christmas? If so, tell about this.

_____

_____

_____

Tell what you know about posadas.

_____

_____

What do you think are the main reasons for the United States and Canada having the same Christmas traditions?

_____

_____

_____

In pairs, select one country for a class project. You may choose one of the above countries. Research how, when, where and why they celebrate Christmas. Make sure you cover any unusual activities and their traditions.

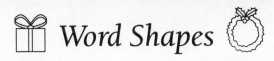

Word Shapes

greetings   holly   Jesus   yuletide   reindeer   stocking   Peace

snowman   Nazareth   shepherds   toys   nativity   angel

tinsel   Bethlehem   December   Christmas   Kings   Rudolph

ribbons

decorations   Santa Claus   goodwill   manger   pudding

Arrange the Christmas words in alphabetical order.

_____ _____ _____ _____ _____

_____ _____ _____ _____ _____

_____ _____ _____ _____ _____

_____ _____ _____ _____ _____

_____ _____ _____ _____ _____

Match the words and write them in the following shapes.

Use the words and make up word pictures; use some of your own Christmas words.

g + [letter] &i

[teapot] f + st

& st [clock] + ing

& st [car]

& k [ring]

[racquet] st + [leek] ek + [nail]

[cloud] ae + d + [ear] ae

Carol Word Find

Complete the titles of these well known Christmas carols and Christmas songs, and place them in the crossword. The words may appear across or down the crossword.

Away in a _____.

_____ the Herald _____ Sing.

Here Comes _____ _____.

_____ Bells.

We Wish You a _____ _____.

Rudolph the _____ Nosed _____.

_____ Night.

Oh, Christmas _____.

The _____ Noel.

O, Holy _____

Frosty the _____.

O, Little _____ of Bethlehem.

Jolly _____ Saint Nick.

Ding Dong Merrily _____ High.

_____ the Night before Christmas.

Little _____ Boy.

Do You _____ What I Hear?

Good _____ _____.

A Winter _____.

God Rest Ye Merry _____.

The _____ and the Ivy.

Joy to _____ _____.

Auld _____ Syne.

The Twelve _____ of Christmas.

We Three _____ of Orient Are.

_____ the Halls.

Once in Royal David's _____.

I'm Dreaming _____ a White Christmas.

Christmas Mapping

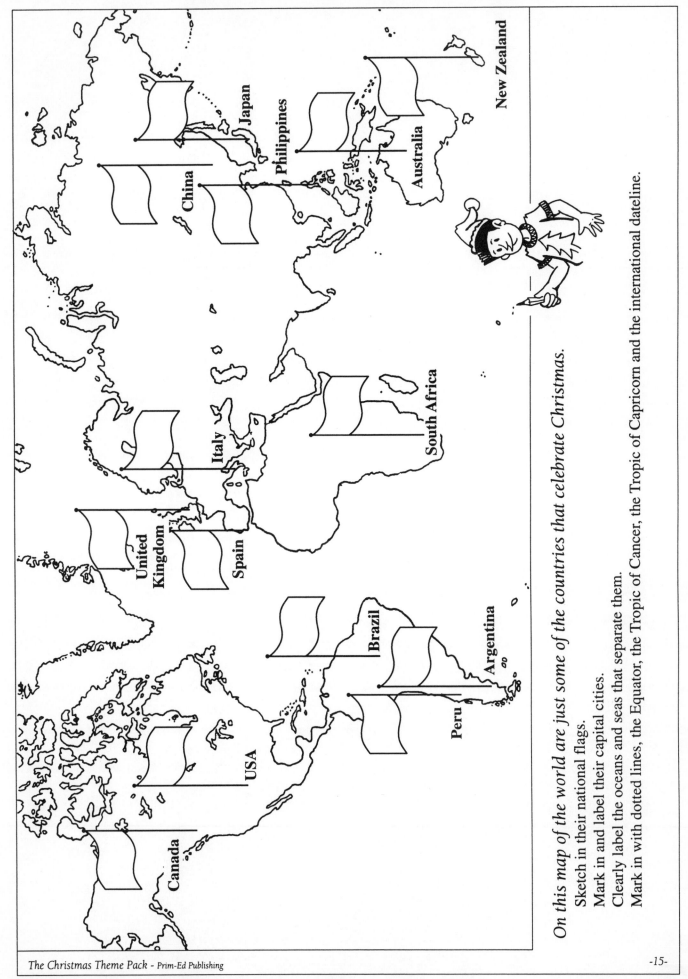

On this map of the world are just some of the countries that celebrate Christmas.

Sketch in their national flags.

Mark in and label their capital cities.

Clearly label the oceans and seas that separate them.

Mark in with dotted lines, the Equator, the Tropic of Cancer, the Tropic of Capricorn and the international dateline.

Christmas Gift List

You have saved your pocket money and have £_____ to spend on presents for your family and friends. Choose what you would like to buy for each person and why.

Who	Present - Price	Why
Mum		
Dad		

Have you gone over your budget? _____

How much more do you need? _____

Your parents will pay you an extra £2 if you wash the car, and £1.50 to wash the dog.

If you did the extra jobs, how long would it take you to earn the money? _____

If you had saved £1.50 every week for a year, how much would you have to spend on the presents? _____

How many Christmas cards can you buy with £30, when the cards cost £2.50? _____

You have £4 to buy stamps.

How many cards can you send, if each card needs a 25p stamp? _____

If you had £80 to spend on Christmas presents and your friend Sam has 50% of the amount you have, how much did you and Sam have altogether? _____

The gift you bought for your mother was more expensive than the one you bought for your sister Jane. Mum's gift cost you £8. Jane's gift cost 60% of Mum's.

How much did you spend on Jane's gift? _____

Christmas Crossword

Across

1. Santa wears one on each foot.
3. Santa's most famous reindeer.
5. One spoke to Mary.
6. Jingle _____, Jingle _____.
8. They pull Santa's sleigh.
9. Used to make snowballs.
11. The night before Christmas.
12. The Wise Men saw it in the East.
13. Rudolph has a shiny red one.
16. The postman delivers these.
20. You hang it up for Santa to fill.
24. _____ New Year.
25. _____ and ivy.
26. We wish you a _____ Christmas.
29. On the end of your feet.
30. One often comes true at Christmas.
32. Reindeers have these.
33. Santa's transportation.
36. Everyone loves to _____ presents.
38. Christmas celebrates his birthday.
40. The First _____.
42. Placed on the Christmas Tree.
43. We _____ Kings of Orient Are.

Down

1. Birth place of Baby Jesus.
2. We have a pine for our _____.
3. Used to tie gifts.
4. Santa gets a _____ from his helpers.
7. Metallic decorations.
9. Brings toys to good children.
10. The sleigh has a full _____.
14. Tiny magical winged female.
15. Hung above the door at Christmas.
17. Meat casserole by another name.
18. The tree looks best a_____.
19. Wrapping for presents.
21. Exchanged with friends and family.
22. Church bells _____ on Christmas Eve.
23. Traditional Christmas dinner is _____.
27. The Christmas season.
28. Children write a gift wish _____.
31. The gifts were _____ from the USA.
33. Seen in the Australian sky at Christmas.
34. Santa's greeting - ho, ho, _____!
35. Theatre entertainment.
37. Christmas cards arrive in the _____.
39. One of Santa's helpers.
41. How many partridges in a pear tree?

Rhyming Limericks

Limericks are funny poems, each line ending with a rhyming word. Use the rhyming words in bold type to complete each poem.

reindeer   pause   Santa Claus   cheer   steer

While chasing a frisky young _____
I heard a loud raucous _____
I took time to _____
To see old _____ _____
Who'd lost Rudolph whose job was to _____

thing   holly   king   sing   jolly

There once was a merry old _____
Who thought that he could _____
One day, feeling _____
He swallowed some _____
And now he can't sing a _____

tree   things   spree   kings   glee

In a Christmas shopping _____
A boy spent money with _____
He bought hundreds of _____
(Some fit for _____)
And he piled them all around the _____

wish   fish   dish   son   done

A young lad who liked to eat _____
Was granted a nice Christmas _____
His dad said, 'Hey _____
Look what I've _____
I've cooked you a nice seafood _____'

star   wise   skies   afar   cries

Three men from the East who were _____
Looked up to the twinkling _____
They saw a bright _____
Shining down from _____
And it led them to a babe's soft _____

🎁 Musical Christmas 🎄

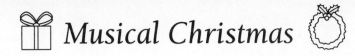

Make some rhyming acrostic poems. Begin each line with the letter given from these Christmas words.

W e love to eat our Christmas meal
R eal turkey, cream and sweets
E verything tastes yummy
A table full of eats
T he hardest part is stopping
H ow can you leave such treats?

S _____
A _____
N _____
T _____
A _____

C _____
H _____
R _____
I _____
S _____
T _____
M _____
A _____
S _____

J _____
E _____
S _____
U _____
S _____

Christmas Context Clues

In the box are some interesting ways of beginning sentences. You shouldn't use the same start for every sentence. Join these beginnings to the following Christmas sentences.

> Gazing up into the night sky ...
> The sound of beautiful carols ...
> The jingling of Christmas bells ...
> Inside the tiny manger ...
> Filled with excitement ...
> The mouth-watering aroma ...
> The bulging Christmas stocking ...
> Rudolph was the only reindeer ...

1. ... a baby lay peacefully in its mother's arms.
2. ... whose nose was shiny and red.
3. ... contained all that the little girl had wished for.
4. ... the Three Wise Men from the East saw a bright star.
5. ... could be heard coming from the little church.
6. ... of Christmas pudding wafted through the air.
7. ... excited the children as they waited expectantly for Santa and his reindeer.
8. ... the children hurried to the Christmas tree to see what gifts they'd received.

Fit the following clues into this story so that it makes sense. Some clues may be used more than once, although avoid beginning or ending sentences with the same answers.

Santa was busy _____. He knew that he

_____ because _____.

The elves were _____ and

_____, painted them bright colours.

Santa's requests had come from _____ but, of course,

only from children in _____.

The long, round-the-world _____. This would take

Santa and his reindeer to _____ and

_____ to millions of children the world over.

1. December 25 was rapidly approaching
2. all around the world
3. making all the toys for Christmas
4. countries where Christianity is practised
5. assembling toys of various shapes and sizes
6. bring joy
7. the far corners of the earth
8. didn't have much time left
9. when they had finished
10. journey was soon to begin

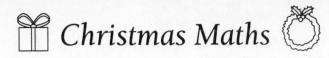

Christmas Maths

Here are the populations of some countries that celebrate Christmas. Show the populations on the bar graph below and then answer the questions that follow.

France (FR)	*56 000 000*	*Switzerland (SW)*	*6 000 000*
Australia (AUS)	*17 000 000*	*Philippines (PH)*	*65 000 000*
New Zealand (NZ)	*4 000 000*	*Great Britian (GB)*	*57 000 000*
Canada (CAN)	*27 000 000*	*United States (USA)*	*253 000 000*

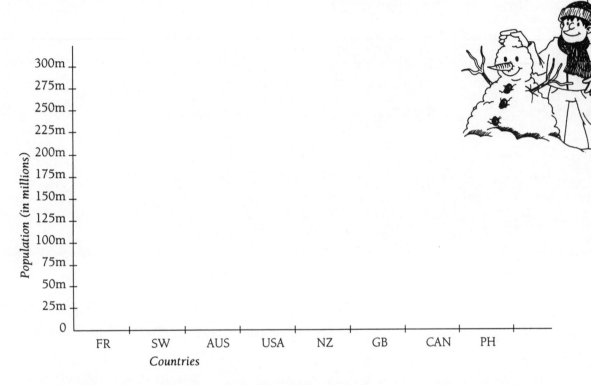

1. Which country has almost seven times the population of New Zealand?
   _____

2. The United States has how many more inhabitants than Great Britian?
   _____

3. Which country has almost four times the population of Australia? _____

4. If the United States had 7 million more inhabitants, its population would be four times that of which country? _____

5. What is the combined population of France, Canada and Great Britain?
   _____

6. The Philippines have six and a half times the population of which two countries combined? _____ _____

7. By how much does the combined populations of the other seven countries fall short of that of the United States? _____

8. Which two countries' populations combined fit into the population of the United States eight times? _____ _____

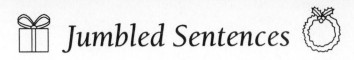

Jumbled Sentences

These sentence were jumbled when Santa tumbled down the chimney.
Help him arrange them so he can move to the next house.

reindeer is **Rudolph** a nosed red-

_____

tree of gifts Christmas it's see the **On** lots to Day nice of at bottom the

_____

Toni **We** Carols Mrs daughter by Smith's Candlelight went with to

_____

was says mother virgin **The** Jesus' Mary bible a that

_____

to Christmas don't spend money have people time some **At** much

_____

stable Mary **When** Bethlehem shelter arrived in Joseph they in and took a

_____

celebrate globe all **Christians** Christmas the around

_____

fifth celebrated the of is day December on twenty- **Christmas**

_____

The last letter of each sentence spells out a Christmas word, reading downwards.
When you have finished, write a sentence, using this word.
Then draw the picture about your sentence.

_____

_____

_____

The Origin of Christmas Cards

In 1843, an English illustrator, Calott Horsley, created the first Christmas card. It looked like a postcard and featured a large family enjoying a Christmas celebration. The message on the card read, 'Merry Christmas and a Happy New Year to You'. About 1 000 of the cards were sold. The custom of exchanging Christmas cards spread throughout Great Britain by 1860.

A German-born Boston printer, Louis Prang, manufactured the first Christmas cards in the United States of America in 1875.

Nowadays, people in Christian nations all around the world give Christmas cards to one another.

Answer the following questions in full sentences.

1. Explain in detail the differences between today's Christmas cards and the first Christmas card.

    _____

    _____

    _____

    _____

2. What do you think are some of the reasons that people exchange Christmas cards?

    _____

    _____

    _____

3. Today's Christmas cards feature a great variety of illustrations on the front cover. What are some of the most common illustrations? (List about ten.)

    _____

    _____

    _____

4. What else beside illustrations can appear on Christmas cards?

    _____

    _____

5. How do you expect the tradition of exchanging Christmas cards spread worldwide?

    _____

    _____

    _____

A Christmas Card

A.

B.

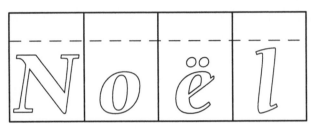

1. A4 card

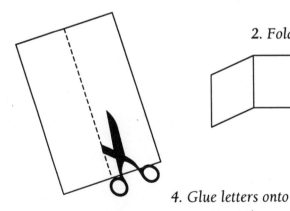

2. Fold

Fold

3. Glue pictures A and B here

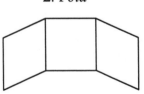

4. Glue letters onto cotton string

5. Attach to the card

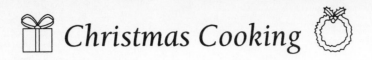# Christmas Cooking

Chocolate Banana Mousse

Ingredients:

300mL   whipping cream
    2   small-medium bananas
200g   dark or milk cooking chocolate (depending on taste)

Method:

Whip cream. Mash bananas. To melt the chocolate, put it in a mug and place it in the microwave for 15-20 seconds at a time. Stir the chocolate frequently until it is smooth and runny. Be careful, it will get very hot!

Mix the cream and the bananas together, add melted chocolate and fold together for a marbled effect.

Serve in dessert cups and decorate with chocolate buds, chocolate shavings, hundreds and thousands or with holly made from red Smarties and mint leaves.

Serve cold.

Christmas Crispies

Ingredients:

100g   butter
130g   raw sugar
230g   mixed fruit and glazed cherries
200g   rice crisp puffs

Method:

Heat butter and sugar in a pan. Slowly mix the chopped dried fruit and glazed cherries into the butter and sugar mixture. Stir constantly until the fruit is soft and well mixed into the butter and sugar.

Add rice crisp puffs and stir well.

Line a baking dish with foil and spread mixture evenly into it. When hardened, cut into pieces about 6 x 2 cm.

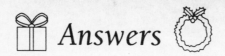

Answers

Christmas Jumbled Cloze - page 5.

List 1 - ribbons, family, three kings, sack, snowman, glitter, stocking, feast, bells. List 2 - Noël, stable, gifts, toys, peace, santa, joy, carols, snow. List 3 - Bethlehem, snowball, Nazareth, mistletoe, christmas tree, sleigh, decorations, tinsel, reindeer.

Cloze - Noël, carols, Christmas tree, tinsel, decorations, glitter, gifts, ribbons, stocking, toys, Santa, reindeer, sleigh, bells, sack, mistletoe, snow, snowman, snowball, feast, family, three kings, stable, Bethlehem, Nazareth, peace, joy.

Nativity Word Sleuth - page 6.

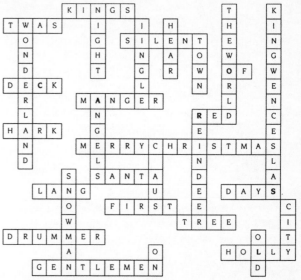

Christmas Code - page 7.

Code Solution - A-24, B-8, C-36, D-25, E-3, F-9, G-15, H-21, I-1, J-45, K-18, L-27, M-4, N-5, O-6, P-7, Q-2, R-10, S-11, T-50, U-12, V-30, W-60, X-20, Y-40, Z-13.

Message - The most important thing at Christmas time is to spread goodwill.

Word Shapes - page 13.

Word Shapes (across) - decorations, December, yuletide, peace, greetings, manger, reindeer, goodwill, Rudolph, pudding, stocking, ribbons, Bethlehem, nativity, Santa Claus, kings, Nazareth, shepherds, angel, tinsel, Christmas, snowman, toys, holly, Jesus.

Word Pictures - glitter, misletoe, kings, stocking, star, feast, reindeer

Jumbled Sentences - page 22.

Word in the boxes - Reindeer

Carol Word Find - page 14.

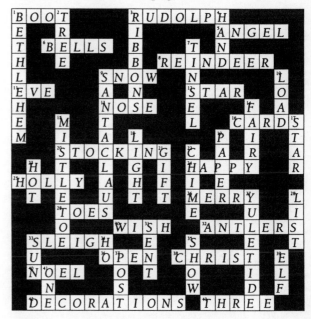

Christmas Crossword - page 17.

Christmas Context Clues - page 20.

Beginning Sentences

1. Inside the tiny manager ... 2. Rudolph was the only reindeer ... 3. The bulging Christmas stocking ... 4. Gazing up into the night sky ... 5. The sound of beautiful carols ... 6. The mouth-watering aroma ... 7. The jingling of Christmas bells ... 8. Filled with excitement ...

Cloze - 3, 8, 1, 5, 9, 2, 4, 10, 7, 6.

Christmas Maths - page 21.

1. Canada 2. 196 000 000 3. Philippines 4. Philippines 5. 140 000 000 6. Switzerland, New Zealand 7. 21 000 000 8. Canada, New Zealand.